Christmas in My Home and Heart

By Robin McGraw

Photographs by Randee St. Nicholas

All photographs of Robin McGraw and her home were taken by Randee St. Nicholas.
Other images: pattern throughout/Copyright emo_o, 2007 Used under license from Shutterstock.com; cover frame/Copyright Vasyl Helevachuk, 2007 Used under license from Shutterstock.com; pg. 6/Copyright Alice, 2007 Used under license from Shutterstock.com; pg. 10/Copyright Ragnarock, 2007 Used under license from Shutterstock.com; pg. 14/Copyright Elena Elisseeva, 2007 Used under license from Shutterstock.com; pg. 18/Copyright Piotr Rzeszutek, 2007 Used under license from Shutterstock.com; pg. 25/Copyright Gastev Roman, 2007 Used under license from Shutterstock.com; pg. 28/Copyright Bretislov Horak, 2007 Used under license from Shutterstock.com; pg. 29/Copyright Audrey M. Vasey, 2007 Used under license from Shutterstock.com; pg. 48/Copyright Mike Flippo, 2007 Used under license from Shutterstock.com; pg. 53/Copyright Vnlit, 2007 Used under license from Shutterstock.com; pg. 64/Copyright Julian Rovagnati, 2007 Used under license from Shutterstock.com; pg. 67/Copyright Baloncici, 2007 Used under license from Shutterstock.com; pg. 88/Copyright Brian Chase, 2007 Used under license from Shutterstock.com; pg. 90/Copyright AMA, 2007 Used under license from Shutterstock.com; pg. 91/Copyright Elena Schweitzer, 2007 Used under license from Shutterstock.com
Project Manager: Lisa Stilwell
Project Editor: MacKenzie Howard
Designed by Susan Browne Design, Nashville, TN

ISBN-13: 978-1-4041-0529-4

Printed and bound in China

www.thomasnelson.com

09 10 11 12 [RRD] 6 5 4 3 2 1

Contents

CHRISTMAS
IN MY
HOME

CREATING MEMORIES *and*
CELEBRATING THE SEASON

Christmas is such an amazing time of the year. It doesn't matter what's going on in life, I still get so excited! I think it's the anticipation of all the season's festivities: putting up decorations; going to parties and get-togethers; creating special family moments; and of course my favorites, the shopping and all of the fabulous food!

As much fun as I have with all of those things, it's always important for me to spend time in deep introspection as the year draws to a close. Time reflecting on the year's events, both good and bad, puts my heart in the right place to be thankful for the blessings in my life. It's a time of forgiveness and renewal, and it helps me start the season with my priorities in order. After all, it's the time with friends and family that I cherish the most.

I know Christmas can be a busy and hectic time of year for many. But in spite of the busyness, it's one of my favorite times of year. It's intended to be a celebration for all people—a time of rejoicing and a time of giving—and I'd love to share with you some of my family's favorite traditions and what we do to capture the true meaning of the Christmas season.

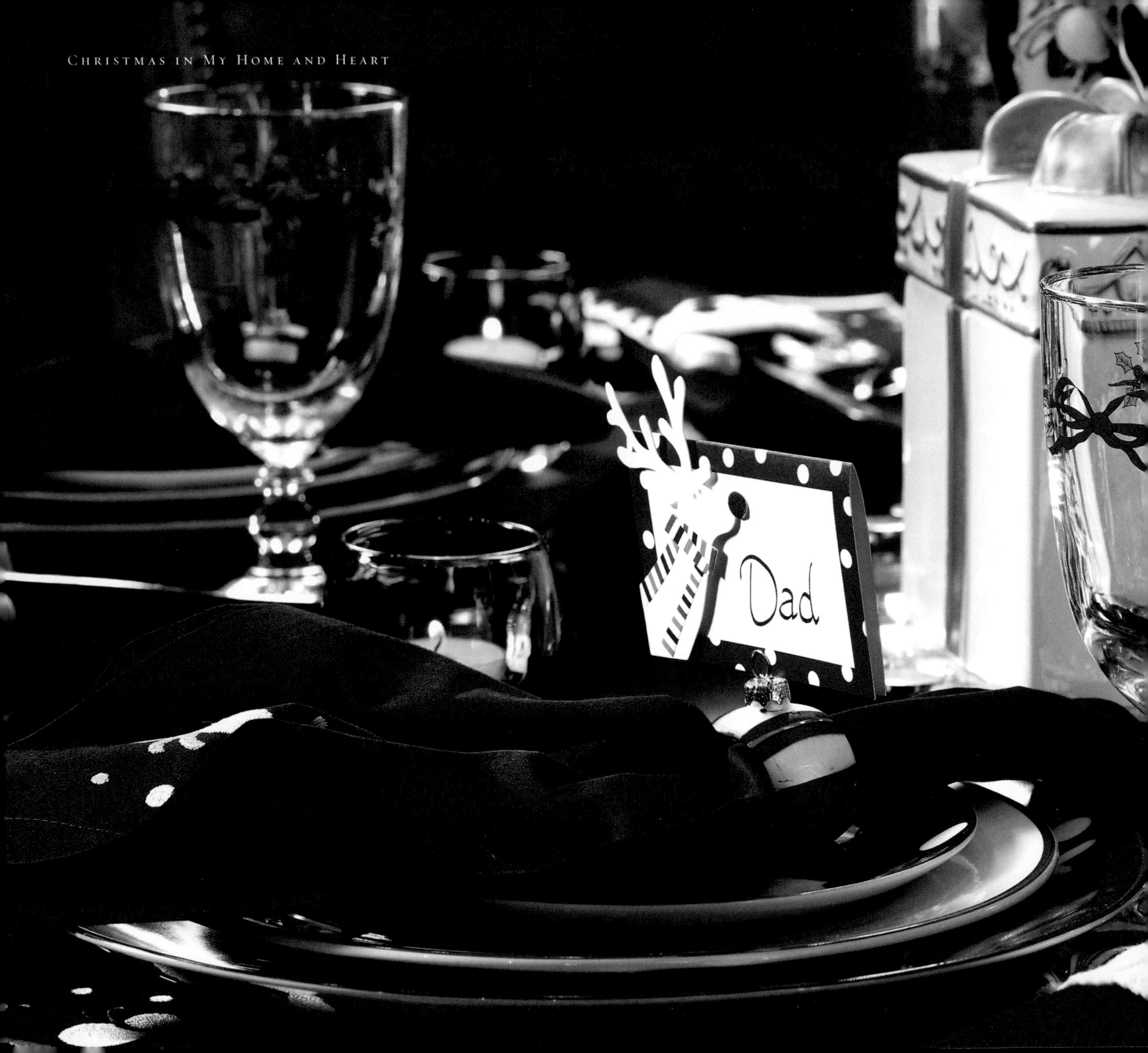
Dad

Hustle and Bustle

The heralding of the holiday season sometimes brings chaos as we try to fit so much into our already busy lives. I really try to keep the stress to a minimum and my schedule realistic while sharing my heart and life with those who are special to me.

PRIORITIZE AND DON'T OVERCOMMIT

I go to extra lengths to make the most out of my time and family visits, but I also try to be careful not to overextend myself because it is too exhausting As much as I want to see everyone and be everywhere, it's just not possible. I've learned that planning ahead and graciously using the word *no* can make a big difference.

In early November, get your calendar or planner and start marking dates. What events have you already been invited to? Which ones reoccur every year? And which ones do you take part in planning? Mark them early to help you decide what you can do and what you need to miss so you're able to enjoy your choices.

When I can't make it to an event or meet a request, I call, send a note, or give flowers to show my sincere appreciation.

Before the season hits, get prepared by creating a stash of Christmas stationery and small gifts for friends, neighbors, and co-workers.

MAKE IT A FAMILY THING

Let's be honest. The holidays can be a lot of work for women. There is so much to be done! So whenever possible, I engage the help of my family and make as many activities as fun as possible. Here are a few things that have become enjoyable family traditions:

CHRISTMAS CARDS: Whether you send a family photo and letter, home-made or store-bought cards, everyone can take part in what can otherwise be a tedious process. Make some cocoa, pop in your favorite Christmas movie, and start an assembly line of signing, addressing, licking, and stamping cards.

GIFT MAKING: Remember all the small gifts you need on hand? Brainstorm about what would be a meaningful gift from your family. Thoughtful thematic baskets can be assembled during another movie night.

A FEW IDEAS:

A Spa Day for Ladies: Fill a trendy container with soaps, scrubs, loofahs, and candles.

Morning Brew: Gather favorite teas, coffees, and cocoas in a tin or a basket. Include a big mug or a travel thermos for the busy commuter.

Golfing Buddy: Collect golf balls, tees, towels, and water bottles in a small cooler.

Goodies: Don't let the holidays pass without baking your favorite treats! Teach your children the family's favorite recipes and bake and decorate your holiday sweets together. Turn up the Christmas carols—and be sure to munch while you work!

BE SATISFIED

I am grateful to have so many special, kind, and wonderful friends and family members in my life, so I do all that I can to share my heart and life with them all throughout the year. Prioritizing, planning, and involving my loved ones can help us get the most out of the season without taking the most out of us. At the end of the day, I have to be feeling good about my decisions, relax, and be satisfied with where I am.

McGraw Family Traditions

I have absolutely loved creating our family traditions over the years. Phillip and I have merged some traditions from our families, and together with our boys, we have started some of our own. From the decorations to the food, there are just some things we have to do every year!

THE DECORATIONS

Decorating is something that a lot of women either love or hate—I love it! It's a great way to unleash my creativity and express myself.

My favorite time is right before Thanksgiving when I break out all of the Christmas decorations and get ready for a decorating fest! I like to have everything in place before our traditional family feast on Thanksgiving Day. For so

many years I spent countless hours decorating the house for Christmas Day, right up until Christmas Eve. I finally realized I spent more time decorating than I did slowing down to enjoy what I'd created! Now I make a point to finish decorating by Thanksgiving Eve, so I can take the time to stop and embrace the coming days and savor my cozy Christmas environment.

My decorating comes from my heart. It is steeped in rich and playful childhood memories of many wonderful Christmases past. Because I love the winter and have a natural desire to retreat to comfort—to sit in front of a warm cozy fire with crackling logs—I'm inspired to create a safe and welcoming haven that reflects our life in many aspects.

From Phillip's and my beginnings in our tiny little apartment in Denton, Texas, to our move out west and in all our homes in between, I've always tried to recreate that warm, comforting Christmas atmosphere that I remember so well while growing up.

I always use traditional red and green. It's my absolutely favorite Christmas color scheme, and it never goes out of style. Pine cone garlands and twinkling lights, velvet bows and shiny ornaments help bring everything to life. I like to dress the foyer with reams of garland twinkling with red and green ornaments. It's so warm and inviting, and that feeling is the first thing I want my guests to experience when they come to our home.

I also like to put lights in potted plants and on mini Christmas trees, and I like to have a Santa and reindeer, with lots of garland streaming around the door and down the steps, all filled with twinkling lights.

THE TREE

I love all kinds of Christmas decorations, but my favorite—and the centerpiece of our home—is the tree. Or trees, I should say! I like to put one in the foyer so it's the first thing you see when you walk through the front door, and then I'll put one in the family room. When the boys were little, I'd put up a miniature tree in each of their bedrooms and let them decorate with whatever theme they wanted.

The Christmas tree is an important symbol of the holiday, and a beautiful way to express that importance in our home, our love for our family, and our spirit. It's been a special place for us to gather as a family, and from my own childhood, to Christmas with Phillip and the boys, memories around the Christmas tree are very special to me.

Decorating the tree is a huge family affair every year. We all get involved in one way or another and the interaction that takes place makes it a lot of fun. I like to start with plenty of lights, so it glows from the inside and creates a magical air about it. Whether it is your tree or your heart, I believe Christmas should shine from within. The joy I receive from setting the season in motion with the boys and their families and friends, remembering those who are not there, and just spending time together sharing stories, joyous laughter, and sometimes tears makes Christmas a precious event every year. Decorating the tree together is such a blessing because it's one of my favorite family traditions.

The first ornament to go on the tree every year is an angel, which I hang in memory of my mother. She passed away on October 21, and as it got closer to that first Christmas without her, I was missing her so much that I went in search of an ornament to hang in memory of her. I found the perfect little angel, standing only four inches tall with short, dark hair, a mauve-colored papier-mâché dress, and little wings on her back. She instantly reminded me of Mother. When the tree goes up, she's the first ornament to go on—and the last one taken off when the tree comes down.

Our family collection of ornaments includes my most cherished pieces—those made by the kids—and all of the pieces that have withstood the years of packing and unpacking. Some of them are tarnished beyond restoration, but they still are held near and dear by us all. Every year we add to our collection, bringing a little

more sparkle, and we rebuild those ornaments that didn't survive their life's journey. I always set aside some time to repair all the little goodies I can't let go of—the homemade ornaments and my favorite reindeer!

I love filling our home with all of our sentimental decorations, the ones the boys made back when they were "boys," and all of our pictures from Christmases gone by. I used to go shopping the day after Christmas because of markdowns, and buy cute Christmas frames for pictures of our family and the boys sitting on Santa's lap. Stopping each year to treasure my sons' pinecone and popsicle stick ornaments and pictures of them when they were little gives me a meaningful perspective of life and time. The years go by so quickly, and these photos are a great reminder of what really matters. What we do at Christmas is not as important as how we do it. No matter what you fill your home with during the season, make sure it all revolves around your family, your values and the love that you share.

Here are a few more McGraw family favorites:

TRAINS

When the boys were little, we began building a train set for each of them. Jason's is old-fashioned, and Jordan's has a circus theme with circus animals in the cars. We've added a new car to the sets every year (and we still do!), so they could take some of our tradition with them into their own adult lives. Jay and his wife put his train around their Christmas tree, but we still have fun running Jordan's around ours.

NUTCRACKERS

I love nutcrackers! I remember my mother having one and just loving it, so when Phillip and I got married, I started my own collection. I've been collecting them for thirty-six years now and probably have about two hundred of them in all! They are so bold and colorful, and the classic Christmas tale that goes with them is so festive. I've always tried to buy ones that reflect our family's experiences that year, especially when the boys were

in sports. I have football, baseball, and basketball nutcrackers. I bought a skier the first year we all went snow skiing as a family. These nutcrackers are a cornerstone of our family decoration celebration during the holidays, and one day I want to share the collection with the boys when they have kids.

NATIVITY SCENES

I love to collect nativity scenes, and I've had about ten different sets over the years. My first nativity set came from Mother, but over the years different pieces have been broken and re-glued so many times that they stay packed and stored away. But I'm always on the lookout for a new set so that when a piece in my current set gets broken, I can bring out the new one for display. I just don't ever want to be without one at Christmas! One tradition I have is to place my mother and father's wedding picture next to the nativity scene, as you can see on the cover of the book.

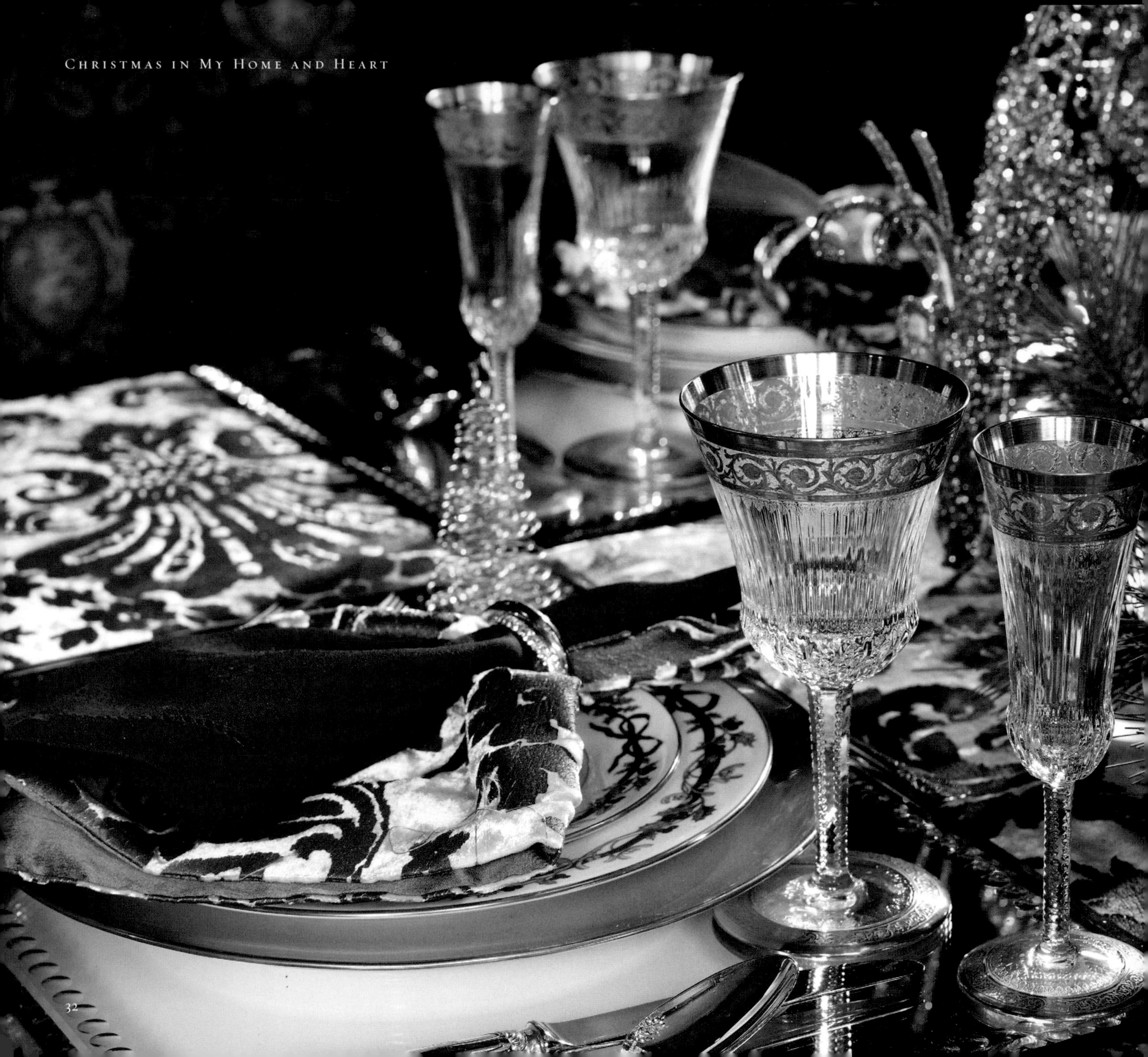

CHINA

I still have my favorite Christmas dinnerware that brings the holiday spirit to every meal. I use it every year for our Thanksgiving Feast to usher in the holiday season, and then I use it every day through the end of December. It's definitely a core part of the season's celebration.

Robin's How-To

Don't let decorating overwhelm you. Sometimes it's easy to get so caught up in "getting it done" or "making it perfect" that it stops being fun! And sometimes, if we are particularly tired or busy, there's a temptation to throw up our hands and forget it entirely! Decorating our homes is about reminding ourselves of the special season we're celebrating and creating pleasant spaces for our friends and family (and ourselves!) to enjoy. Whether you're adding a few simple touches like candles and wreathes or tackling a total home makeover, just be sure to keep the process enjoyable. Don't extend your time or your budget—both will leave you stressed. And whatever you do, make sure there's time to savor your efforts when you're done.

AND THEN THERE'S THE FOOD!

When it comes to food, we've got a plan, and that's to have lots of it! If there's anything that gets me excited, it's preparing and eating delicious food! I don't think there's any better time to enjoy food and fellowship than during the holidays.

I take great pride in digging into the family arsenal of our ultimate favorites. I make the time to prepare favorite meals and goodies for everyone from pot roasts to cookies and more cookies. Our family recipe for almond cookies is the best—it's so simple and easy to make. And then there are Mother's noodles! She started a tradition of making these creamy wide egg noodles by combining the noodles with butter, onions, sour cream. It's such a simple dish, but it's so delicious and something we have only at Christmastime. They are one of my favorite comfort foods, satisfying and always good for the soul.

The month leading up to Christmas Day, as the boys have grown, I've attempted to recruit them and their friends for fresh baked cookies and snacks or even for dinner before they'd take off to their own holiday parties. These invitations provided wonderful opportunities to connect and make memories, not just with the boys, but with their friends too.

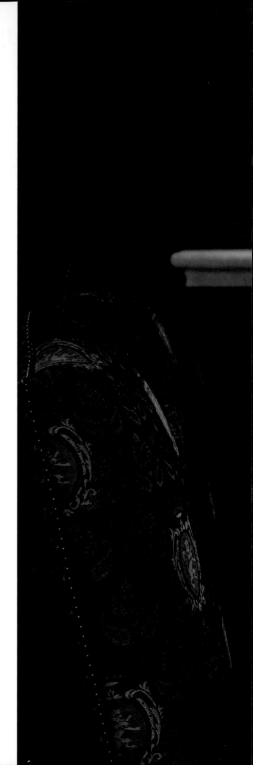

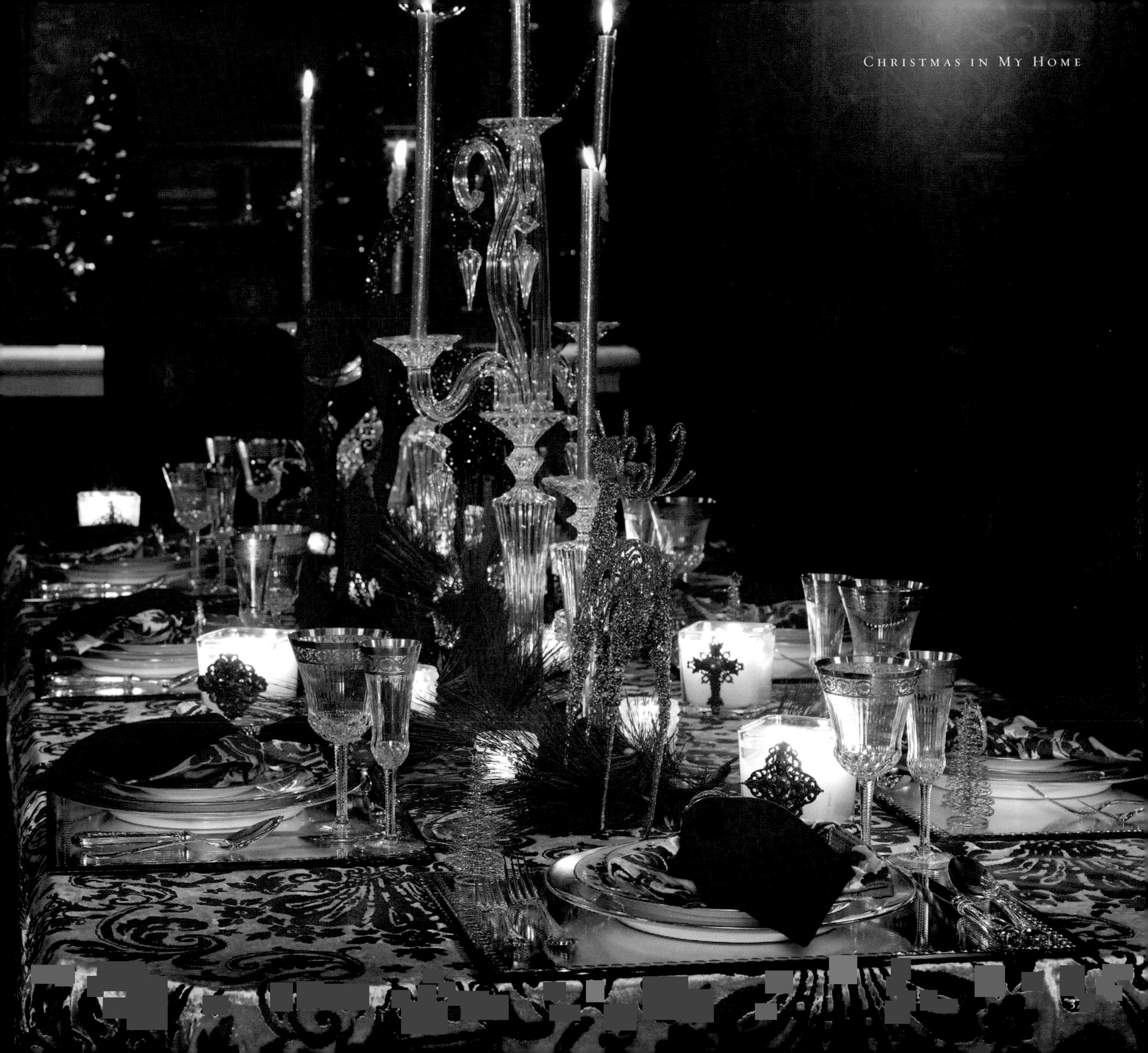

[redacted]

THE MENU AT THE McGRAWS

On Christmas Eve and Christmas Day, the family is always together. Grandma Jerry, Phillip's mother, alternates her visits with us, so she's here for Thanksgiving one year and Christmas the next.

Every year on Christmas Eve, we have baked potato soup, a recipe I got from an old Betty Crocker cookbook that my mother gave me years ago, and HoneyBaked Ham sandwiches. We do it every year. It is simple to put together and such a delicious combination. Then on Christmas morning Phillip makes his traditional biscuits with ham for breakfast for everyone. He makes that time for us delightful and heartwarming.

Our traditional Christmas dinner is prime rib. We love to have all the vegetables we can possibly fit on the table, including roasted potatoes and carrots. It is a cornucopia of treats! Over the years I've loved cooking the whole dinner myself, but now I enjoy sharing the time with Jay's wife, Erica.

CHRISTMAS ALMOND COOKIES

We make these delightful little cookies every year. They're my favorite, and they're so easy to make. I love to turn on the Christmas music and get busy in my kitchen!

INGREDIENTS:

1 1/2 cup butter, room temperature

3/4 cup powdered sugar

3 teaspoons vanilla extract

3 cups flour

1/4 teaspoon salt

1/2 cup slivered almonds

An additional 1 cup powdered sugar
to roll cookies in

PREPARATION:

Combine the softened butter, ¾ cup powdered sugar, and vanilla at high speed with a mixer. In a separate bowl combine flour and salt. Slowly add the seasoned flour to the butter until well incorporated. Fold in the slivered almond.

Gently roll the dough into one-inch balls. Place the balls on a lightly greased cookie sheet about 2 inches apart.

Bake in a 300° oven for about 30 minutes. Cookies should be crisp but not golden. Roll the warm cookies in the powdered sugar.

ROBIN'S FAMILY RECIPE CHEESY NOODLE CASSEROLE

INGREDIENTS:

2 cups sour cream

2 cups cottage cheese

1/4 cup minced onions

1/2 cup melted butter

1 tbl Worcestershire sauce

6 dashes Tabasco

1 tbl salt

2 tsp pepper

16 oz.-package wide egg noodles (cooked al dente)

PREPARATION:

Cook egg noodles according to package directions. Place in a large mixing bowl and set aside.

Sautee the ¼ cup minced onions in ½ cup melted butter. Cook until onions are translucent. Combine cooked noodles, sautéed onions, sour cream, cottage cheese, Worcestershire sauce, Tabasco, salt, and pepper. Toss until ingredients are thoroughly incorporated.

Pour the noodle mixture into a greased casserole dish. Bake uncovered in a 350° oven for 30 minutes. The top will be slightly golden. Serve immediately.

Robin's How-To

Gourmet meals are always a treat, but sometimes life is easier if you limit the number of times you have to prepare them during the holidays. If dinner on Christmas Day is a four-course affair, soups and sandwiches or appetizers are great options for Christmas Eve. Whenever you can, allow friends and family to bring sides and desserts. Sharing the cooking duties makes for a wide variety of goodies, and it takes some pressure off you.

If you can, involve your children in your culinary exploits. When they're young, the cooking may take more time, but as they get older, their help really will be a time saver. Plus, it equips them with fantastic holiday memories and the ability to carry special family recipes and traditions into their own homes. Phillip's and my traditions and favorite foods are special combinations of things from our own lives growing up, and I love that the boys will be able to share them with their families.

Christmas Then and Now

Life is constantly changing; no matter who we are or where we live, we all deal with change on a regular basis. Our family is no different. But I have chosen to learn to see change as an adventure and an opportunity to thrive, not just survive. And as a part of that thriving, I take every opportunity to learn from my past experiences, relish my memories, and make the most of my circumstances. Especially during the holidays!

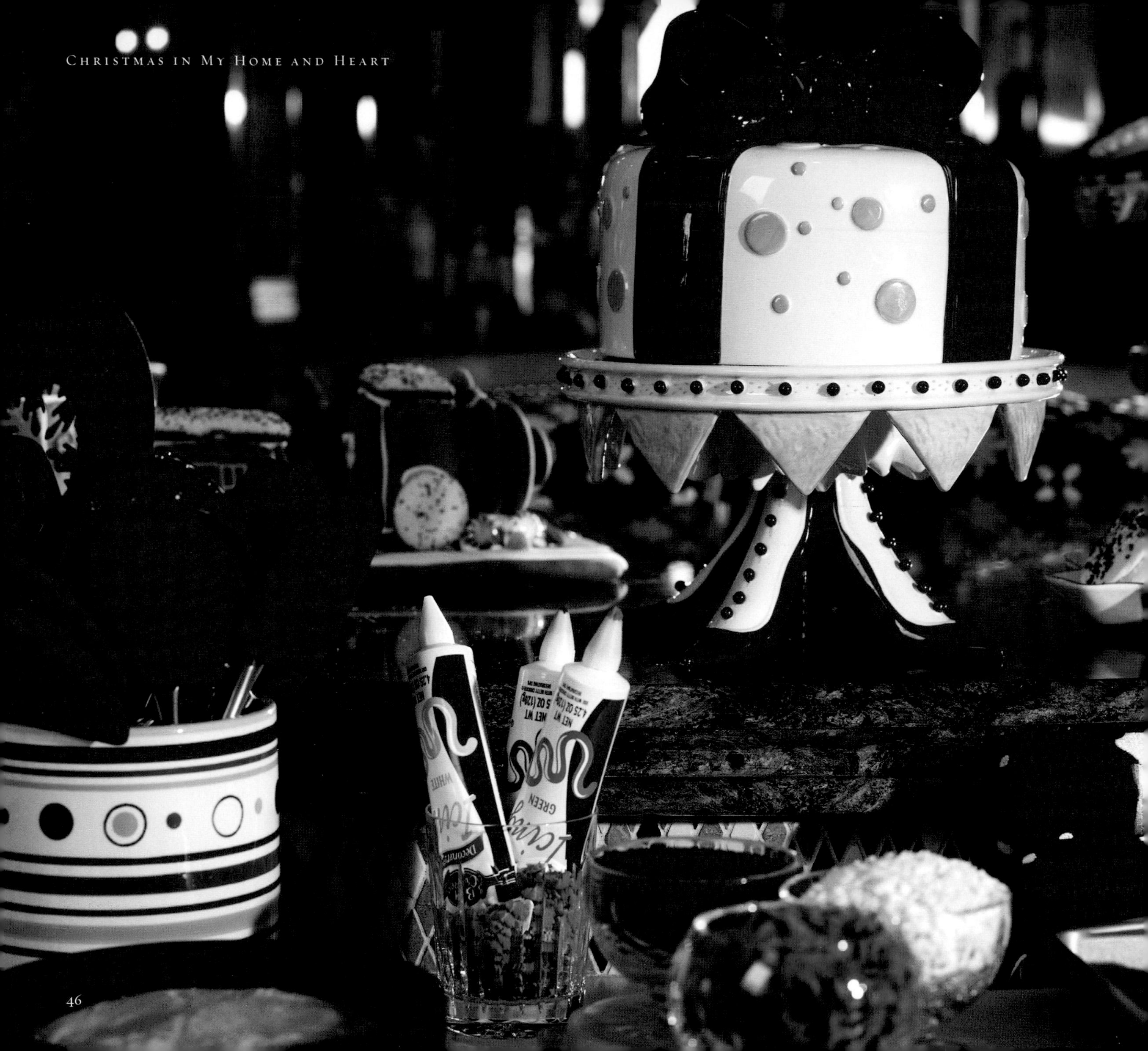
NET WT
4.25 OZ (120g)
WHITE
GREEN

CHRISTMAS PAST

When I was growing up, I was blessed to have a very loving family. We never had much materially; in fact I never had store-bought clothes until after high school, but our Christmases were still very special. Instead of lots of gifts, Mother would find one perfect gift that she knew we really wanted. She had a tradition of not putting our gifts under the tree until Christmas Eve, so whenever she'd leave to go the grocery store or run an errand, my sister would jump at the chance to try and find where she hid the gifts. Her snooping would make me a nervous wreck, but I couldn't resist the fun when she'd call out, "Here they are!" One time my sister found my Barbie Dream House hidden in a closet under my mother's robe, and when I saw it, I just couldn't believe my eyes. I was so excited I ran out and told my other sister but, to my demise, she told mother what happened after she got home. Not surprisingly my gift wasn't under the tree that Christmas morning! So I learned the hard way that it's not worth it to snoop for presents. This story has a good ending though. Mom brought my Dream House out three days later for my birthday! I think these early experiences (and my precious mother's uncanny ability to make everything special whether we had money or not) taught me the joy of giving and receiving.

When Phillip and I were first married, we too were on a very tight budget. I remember one year when we only had $10 to spend on each other's Christmas presents. Times were lean, and that was just the way it was. But I had learned well from my mom that lean times don't mean things can't be special. That year we had a picnic in front of the fireplace for Christmas dinner, and it was so perfect. When we exchanged gifts, he had gotten me a wooden candleholder that held three candles. I was so touched by

Phillip's thoughtfulness. Nothing could have replaced it, and to this day Phillip and I still have our own private Christmas ceremony. Sometimes, making it through the lean times makes the plentiful times all the more meaningful.

CHRISTMAS ON A BUDGET

Christmas on a budget can actually be really fun. I spent many years with my holidays falling under a tight budget. I embraced the challenge of getting the most out of my hard-earned savings and turned it in to a positive experience! Here are a few of my favorite tips:

- Homemade ornaments are the best! I remember stringing popcorn and cranberries.

- Hanging ready-made gift bows in place of ornaments is very festive and sweet.

- Thrift stores are a great source for holiday linens and tableware.

- Poinsettias are amazing and last for months and months.

- Clipping branches from evergreens in your own yard can be a great way to adorn packages or create centerpieces.

- Instead of buying for everyone, suggest drawing names and putting a price limit on the gift. Or you can draw names and make gifts. Put a limit on supply costs like five or ten dollars.

- Crafting with friends is a fun way to spend holiday time together and make the most out of your pocketbook.

- Make gift certificates to do someone's chores for a week. For your spouse, you can make certificates for back massages, a night off from cooking and kid detail, or a complimentary car wash. This is a neat gift that only requires time and is always appreciated.

- Create a cookbook of all your family's favorite recipes or a photo album of a special event.

AND THEN THERE WERE FOUR

The boys' arrival was such a blessing. Starting our own family traditions gave Christmas even deeper meaning, although they really weren't much different from our family traditions when I was growing up. I think my funniest memory is that on Christmas morning we would have to wake up the boys! All I can remember as a little girl was waiting for my parents to get up!

Leading up to Christmas Day, we'd let the boys open gifts from friends and extended family as they were dropped off or delivered in the mail. That just kept the excitement going throughout the month. But the tradition for opening our gifts has always been to spend December 23 doing all the wrapping at once. Then we set all of the gifts out on Christmas Eve, so not one of ours was opened until Christmas morning after breakfast. We are adamant about Christmas not just being about the presents. Plus, we love the overnight transition of having no gifts, to seeing everything under the tree at once!

We've had so much fun over the years surprising our sons. The best part was seeing their little faces light up! One year we gave Jay a go-cart which was too big to fit under the tree, so I ran a big red ribbon from the doorknob on his room that went all the way downstairs and out to the garage. We had piles of

red ribbon that circled the adorable little machine. Another year we wanted to

surprise Jordan with a pinball machine, so we made him bunk up with

Jay on Christmas Eve. We ran ribbons from his bed to his own

room; the suspense that year was incredible. He had no

clue what it was going to be!

Another family favorite of ours with the boys was

the annual Christmas lights competition. When we lived

in Dallas, our community had a lights competition every

year, and we'd sneak out and patrol the neighborhood to

see what everyone was doing. Then we'd keep adding more and

more lights! We would travel out and tour the lights and decorations in

the different neighborhoods to get ideas. We won that competition four years

in a row! The grand prize was a piece of a Christmas village, and the year that we

didn't win, Phillip went out and bought me another piece for our little village

collection. Lights patrol with the boys was the best!

Some things never change . . .

Although we haven't done lights patrol in a while, there are some things we're just never too old for! Christmas music and Christmas movies are on all the time during the holidays. We really enjoy spending the time with the kids watching films and preparing meals. Just about anything can turn into a major family event full of joy, laughter, and great memories.

Christmas music is particularly near and dear to our hearts. When our son Jordan was in first grade, he learned to play the piano. His first Christmas song was "Silent Night" and I will never forget him serenading us with that sweet carol. He's now a professional musician, and we are so proud.

MY FAVORITE THINGS

- During Christmas we visit numerous churches and see the holiday programs. Phillip loves the music, and the programs are truly beautiful.

- My favorite Christmas song is "O Holy Night."

- I can't wait to have grandchildren and share our time-honored traditions with them!

- Christmas is a great time to break out the old photo albums and reminisce about all the joy and amazing life experiences I have had and have shared with my devoted friends. Those funny, outrageous, and silly moments have helped mold me as a woman and have tested my character to its limits! These building blocks of my life are irreplaceable.

As women, we set the tone in the homes and lives of our families. This is not a burden; it's a privilege! I hope that wherever you are and whatever you've experienced, you can take the time at Christmas to create a wonderful haven for your family and friends—even if the only thing you have to offer is a heart full of love. Trust me, that's enough.

CHRISTMAS
IN MY
NEIGHBORHOOD

CREATING *and*
SPREADING HOSPITALITY

Showing hospitality to friends, family, neighbors, and even strangers can be a wonderful gift, and it's one of my favorite things to do. I love making someone feel special, and that can happen when all I do is offer a steaming cup of cocoa! Through the years, I have been blessed by so many people whose kind acts of thoughtfulness have touched my heart. Because of those kindnesses, I make a point to not get so bogged down with holiday busyness that I don't have time to extend joy to others.

One of my favorite ways to share the season's joy is to welcome people into my home. . . .

Entertaining

I love entertaining, especially during the holidays! I know it's something that can get hectic and sometimes be a burden, but as long as we keep our priorities in order and our task list manageable, it is such a pleasure. I particularly love intimate family-style parties where we can catch up with friends, eat our favorite goodies, and share our plans for the coming year.

Our parties always have a theme, and on these special occasions I really get to express myself, from designing and making the invitations all the way to planning the finest details of the menu. Remember, the fun should always outweigh the work, and let everything be a unique expression of you. Whether you focus on the food, the centerpieces, or the activity—choose things you love to do that you also know will make your guests feel welcome and engaged.

HERE ARE JUST A FEW OF
MY FAVORITE PARTY IDEAS:

I like to hire a photographer to get lots of pictures, and later I create little photo albums to send to the guests. If a photographer is not in the budget, hand your digital camera to an older child or teen, particularly if they have artistic aspirations. Show them how to use the camera and caution them to be professional and to not wear out the guests. Pay them a few bucks for a job well done. They'll love it!

We do karaoke, games, whatever comes to mind for that particular occasion. These activities can be hugely entertaining, and they're also easy for guests to contribute. There are always a few in the crowd who make games a really funny experience. (And I'm often shocked that you can be friends with people for a while and not know how beautiful their voices are until they sing karaoke!) Let guests know in advance to bring their favorite game, and there will be a wide selection for everyone to choose from.

And my golden rule for guest lists is this: Never invite anyone who makes you feel bad. Celebrations are exactly that—celebrations. They are to be times of joy. They are not times for you to be feeling obligated to include those who have a history of bringing you down. It is your right to support your own well-being in an event.

Robin's How-To

If it's a family occasion, there are certain people you just can't leave off the guest list whether they're fun to be with or not! For instance, I am fortunate to have fantastic in-laws, but I know that not everyone is that blessed. So to keep the peace and your sanity, simply don't offer to host the family event. Be cordial and helpful; offer to do what you can to bring food, beverages, or supplies. Show up with the family, help out with preparation and cleanup, and then go home and rest before your nerves are shot!

EASY IDEAS FOR SMALL GROUPS

If you've never done a thematic party, here is a really fun idea that can be used during the holidays or anytime during the year:

CHOCOLATE!

This one is especially fantastic for a girls-only affair! Host a tasting of all sorts of decadent chocolate—white, milk, and dark chocolate treats in all sorts of varieties. Chocolate fountains have become very affordable, and a great way to share recipes is to ask all your girlfriends to bring their favorite chocolate dessert. A woman can never have too many ways to eat chocolate!

How about Christmas music? Everyone who comes over for festivities brings a favorite Christmas CD. Each CD gets played over the course of the get-together.

CHRISTMAS LIGHTS TOUR

When you've got a small gathering of intimate friends, pack up some travel mugs of cocoa and tins of goodies and pile into a van for an evening of Christmas lights! Pick someone who is most familiar with the best spots, and take a tour of your area. It's a fun way to get ideas and see how extravagantly some people decorate. Don't forget the Christmas music and bundle up!

PROGRESSIVE DINNERS

This one is a lot of fun! During a progressive dinner, one couple plans to host appetizers; another, the main course; and a third, the dessert. The group can travel en masse to each home. It's an easy way to share the burden of food preparation, a great time for fellowship, and a perfect opportunity to see everyone's home dressed for the holidays!

If planning elaborate affairs just does not work for your time schedule or family situation (trust me, we've all been there), there are still a lot of great ways to plan meaningful events that everyone will enjoy.

EASY IDEAS FOR LARGE GROUPS

ORNAMENT EXCHANGE POTLUCK

Have an ornament party—even the guys can join in on this fun! Everyone brings a potluck dish and a wrapped ornament with no name attached. (No one knows who brought what.) When you're ready to begin, everyone sits in a circle, and the first person picks a gift and opens it. The next person can either take the first person's ornament or pick one from under the tree. Keep going this way, trading up to three times per person. Everyone will soon discover just how possessive of an ornament (in a fun way) folks can get!

CHRISTMAS COOKIE SWAP

Plan a coffee-and-dessert party where guests brings a favorite dessert and note cards with the recipe on them. Everyone is responsible for only one item, and everyone gets to sample a large variety of yummy snacks. And with the recipe cards, everyone gets to take home some of their favorites!

Connecting with Old Friends

Christmas is the perfect time of year to connect with friends old and new and to send out updates on your life. Entertaining is a great way to catch up, but many of us have friends and family living thousands of miles away. Sending out cards with letters and photos is a great way to keep these special people in your life up-to-date. And I love getting them in return! I remember when we would send out photos of the boys every year, and today I love getting photos of our friends' children and grandchildren, hearing stories of how God has been working in their lives, and being able to celebrate together despite the miles, even if it's just through the mail.

Robin's How-To

CHRISTMAS LETTER DO'S AND DON'TS

DO: Keep it brief. About one typed page is enough..

DON'T: Write a memoir. If you hit four pages, start a blog!

DO: Share the year's highlights. If you've had a milestone, taken a fabulous trip, or

been blessed by a landmark opportunity, share away!

DON'T: Exaggerate or brag (at least not too much!)

DO: Be honest. If the year was rough, it's okay to say so.

DON'T: Divulge private or overly detailed information. Be especially careful

to not speak negatively of others.

Reaching Out to Neighbors

I can remember many times throughout my life when we were just settling in after moving from here to there, and I would be blessed with gifts of house-warming during the holidays by our new neighbors. I was always so touched by their kind thoughts and by that spirit of giving selflessly and truly expecting nothing in return except to ease someone else's burden. These acts of kindness spurred a family tradition to always show hospitality to our neighbors, remembering it's not what joy I receive in giving, it is spreading joy for others to experience.

Sometimes starting little traditions with long-distance friends creates a warm, sentimental bond that can last for decades! And it's so fun to anticipate the arrival of those special tokens of love. Phillip has an old friend from college named Ken Petruck. They were roommates when they played football, and every year for the last forty years he has sent a flowering plant to the house for Christmas. We have always been so touched that even after this length of time, he still remembers us at Christmastime. His tradition is truly beautiful and truly appreciated.

There are so many ways to reach out to neighbors during the Christmas season and all year around. Here are a few I try to keep in mind:

- Is anyone new to the neighborhood? Can I take them a housewarming gift to make them feel as welcome as I've been made to feel over the years?

- Is there a single-parent family who could use some help? What could I take to them or do for them that will ease their holiday season?

- Have any of the families had a particularly rough year? What could I do to brighten this season?

- And, finally, if you just want to welcome everyone, host a drop-in party with snacks and hors d'oeuvres to draw in and see as many neighbors and friends as you can.

Christmas
IN MY
THOUGHTS

CHERISHING MEMORIES *with*
LOVED ONES

Like so many things in our lives, our thoughts and our attitudes help determine how an event or circumstance may turn out. Christmas is no different. I always make an effort to focus on the positive, to focus on the good things in every facet of my life, and then to calmly and prayerfully try to figure out the bad ones. Sometimes we need to do this even with something as wonderful as Christmas!

Christmas in My Childhood

My mother was a major contributor to teaching me this life lesson of focusing on the good instead of the bad. In fact, she did this almost to a fault. We didn't really have much materially, but that didn't deter my mother, and it didn't ever seem to get the best of her. Even though she didn't receive expensive presents or fancy gifts, she still always managed to make Christmas a joyous occasion for us kids. Although my childhood was often very uncertain, I credit my mother with keeping Christmas a very exciting time for me.

My mother was so into the holidays; she truly emulated the Christmas spirit.

Remembering Loved Ones

When lives are wrought with despair—when we are mourning lost loved ones, estranged spouses, wayward children—it can be heart wrenching at times to even try to muster a smile. In my life, even under the worst circumstances, I prayed for healing and tried to focus on happy memories and the hope I have in God.

Because the holidays are such an important family time, they remind us in one way or another of those who are no longer with us. Even though those feelings are sometimes painful, I always try to turn it around and remind myself that they are in a better place, and I think of the many blessings those I loved so dearly brought to my life.

Every year I go to church and light a candle for my mother because she passed so close to the holidays. Lighting a candle is my way of honoring and remembering her spirit. That first year without her was particularly rough. We all pulled together and leaned on one another. It felt like a miracle to make it through. At times like this you realize just how important family really is. I find it quite comforting to know now that I was never alone during those trying times. I felt God's presence in every thought and fond memory of my mother.

The births both of my boys were true miracles in my life, especially with Jordan being born the day my mother had passed exactly two years later. I always felt that Mom was with me and that Jordan's arrival just before the holidays was a breath of renewal for that challenging time. I felt Mother's presence that day, and I knew my lovely baby boy was a gift from God. Sometimes just seeing his face is a special reminder of her.

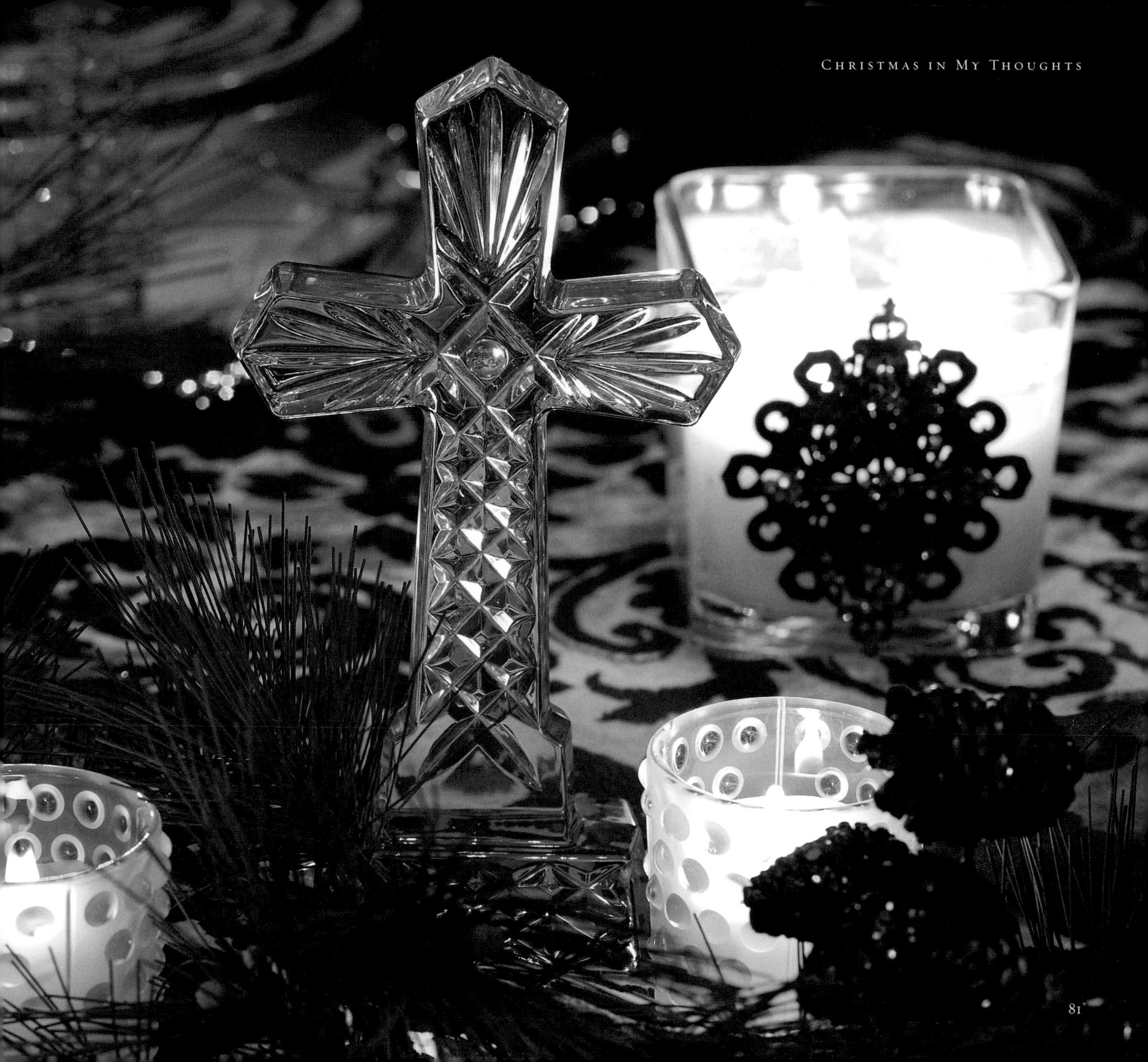

Finding ways to honor loved ones who have passed can be a way to bring healing during the holidays:

- Plant a tree, flowers or a rosebush in your yard, something that stays with you year-round, and something you can decorate during the holidays.

- Prepare their favorite foods in their honor. Sometimes the simplest things keep the spirit alive.

- Dedicate a poinsettia or their favorite flower arrangement in their honor to display in church one Sunday.

- Have a "Remember when . . ." time at one of your family gatherings. Take turns sharing one of your favorite memories of that person.

CHRISTMAS
IN MY
SERVICE TO OTHERS

REACHING OUT
TO OTHERS IN NEED

Our Greatest Work, Our Greatest Gift

I get particularly inspired as the holidays approach every year and I witness the community coming together, practicing more forgiveness, showing more tolerance, and embracing the constant reminder: give to others.

Phillip and I have made it a priority in our lives to give to others, and we have taught our sons to do the same. Giving back is at the core of our family values. At times giving simply involves a kind word, a smile, or an afternoon offering nothing but time. Sometimes our giving is a huge event with a national organization, and other times it's as simple as noticing that the woman next door could use a hand. Sometimes the smallest acts of giving can completely change your life. . . .

SERVICE

In 2004 Phillip and I hosted a party for the children and family members of our soldiers serving in Iraq, and it was a life-changing event for us. It is almost impossible to describe the pure joy of knowing we were able to bring laughter and joy to the holidays for those amazing children and their families on that special day. The spirit of giving and alleviating our fellow man's burden reminds me constantly that the need for God's presence and His blessings are, at times, felt deeply within our hearts. It is my duty as a woman, wife, and mother to be of service to others.

I was honored to share a greeting from one of America's finest, a soldier abroad. It was a message of hope and love and inspiration to his wife and children. As I pored over the words, which I had the privilege of delivering to this lovely woman and her children, I was barely able to contain myself. It was one of the single most moving experiences I've ever had. I was able to share with the world and those watching to never give up hope and to know that God blesses us all each and every day.

These were monumental events Phillip and I were humbled to take part in, but beyond that, service is a way of life. It's having a willing heart that is ready to reach out at any given opportunity. If your eyes are opened and your heart is willing, opportunities to serve are everywhere!

SECRET SANTAS

If there's anything better that giving, it's giving anonymously and leaving people surprises!

When we lived in Wichita Falls, Phillip had an office in town. There was an alleyway behind the building where he parked. Every day when he went in to work, there was a woman playing with a little boy out in the alley. They'd scurry away when the cars rolled in. One day as Christmas was drawing close, Phillip stopped the young boy and asked him when he was going to put up his Christmas tree. The boy explained that his mom couldn't afford one and that they weren't going to put one up this year.

Then Phillip asked, "What do you want for Christmas this year?" He had no answer.

So we arranged to send the boy and his aunt and mother out for pizza one day. While they were away, we got to work! We set up a tree, decorated it, put up flashing twinkle lights, and left all kinds of goodies for the aunt and mother. Then we picked up a bunch of Dallas Cowboys memorabilia for the boy and left a ham on the table. We rushed out to wait for their return. We could see the Christmas lights from Phillip's office; we were so excited! As they walked up the little boy started yelling, "Mommy, look at the lights! The lights!" The excitement was thrilling. Making a difference in a stranger's life is fulfilling in a way the touches your soul. The core of our joy is always about the children. Anytime you can touch the life of a child, you take part in changing the world.

Another time when I worked as an industrial engineer technician, Thanksgiving was drawing close, and I was down in the plant conducting efficiency time studies. I was in with the technicians and monitoring their work. I struck up a conversation with a young woman. She revealed she wasn't too excited about the holidays coming, and I came to find out that she was a single mother with three kids. She wasn't even going to celebrate Thanksgiving that year because she just couldn't afford it.

Oh yes, she will be celebrating! I thought.

I was able to inconspicuously glean some important information from our conversations . . . *So what kind of car do you drive? And the color?*

Well, wouldn't you know the day she left for the holiday there were six bags of groceries—a complete Thanksgiving meal in the back seat of her car! She kept trying to get my confession but I never let on. My joy was in the giving. Seeing new hope swell up in someone after they've received an unexpected gift, and knows that they are cared for and loved, is priceless.

WORTHY ORGANIZATIONS

🌸 We've worked with Toys for Tots for many years. Donating to this organization is as simple as dropping off one new, unwrapped toy. The U.S. Marine Corps is in charge of this program, and their goal is to reach out to youngsters with a message of hope.

🌸 Phillip and I are also national spokespersons for CASA, the Court Appointed Special Advocates program. Anytime we can do anything to improve the life of a child, we are compelled to do it. We dedicate nearly all of our philanthropic efforts to children in need. Our mission is to reach out and touch a child's life all year long, but especially at Christmastime.

🌸 Another great organization is Operation Christmas Child. The organization Samaritan's Purse collects shoe boxes full of gifts for boys and girls and distributes them to children in need all over the world. This is a very cost-effective way for you and your children to help.

A Tradition of Giving

Phillip and I have found that a great way to keep the focus off the presents and the stuff at Christmas was to get our boys involved in giving. This is such a meaningful way for families to bond together, and giving is such an important lesson for children. It teaches them from an early age what Christmas is really about.

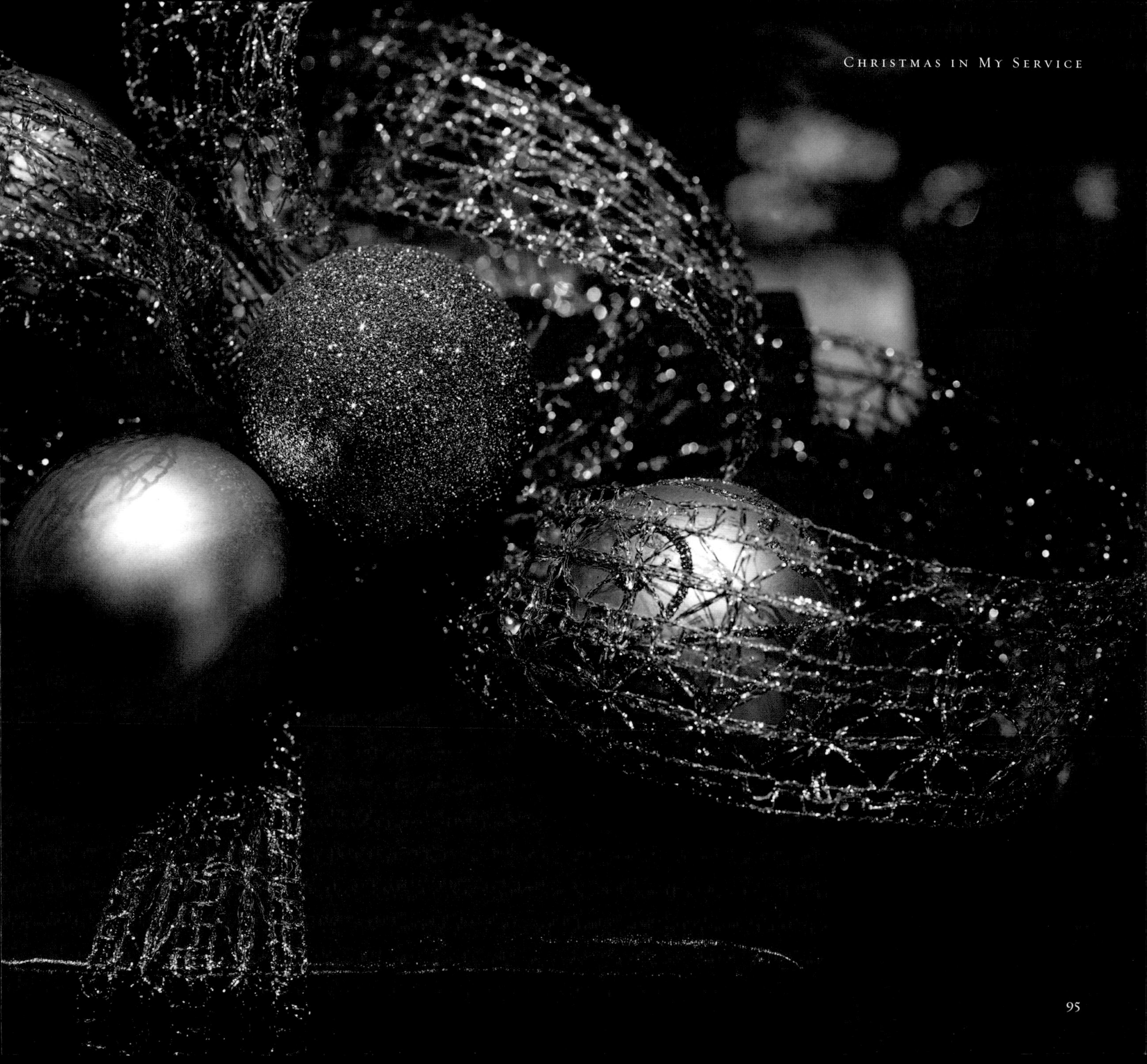

Robin's How-To

I know how tight money can be, especially around the holidays, but sacrificing to help others will pay off big rewards of inner gratification. One thing I suggest is for families to "adopt" another family for Christmas. You can do this through the Salvation Army's Angel Tree program or even through your local social services. Pick a family similar to your own and get your kids involved. For example, if you have a boy and girl, maybe adopt a family with a boy and girl. Involve the kids in the shopping and let them help pick out gifts for the family. This involvement makes the experience really personal for them. Adopting a family is one Christmas tradition that will never get old.

CHRISTMAS
IN MY
HEART

DRAWING NEAR
TO GOD

Because Christmas is such a busy time of year, we can sometimes get too caught up in good things. Yes, I said good things! Even when we're giving of our time and resources, when we're working for a worthy cause, when we're helping others, we still need to stop and reflect upon the Source of all giving, the Source of all goodness. All good things come from God, and we give because He gave to us the ultimate gift: the gift of His Son Jesus.

The Greatest Gift

The Christmas story in Luke is definitely my favorite passage in the Bible. Every time I read it, I am inspired by Mary and Joseph and how they overcame trials, how they persevered despite much adversity, and how they faced the tough decisions they had to make to ensure the safe delivery of our holy Son. They remained steadfast and, regardless of the consequences, they continually moved forward in fulfilling God's plan for them and for His Son. They taught kindness and compassion to all who witnessed them, and no matter how they were perceived by those who did not accept them, they knew in their hearts and in their spirits what was right. It's because of this the world was able to receive the greatest gift of all time.

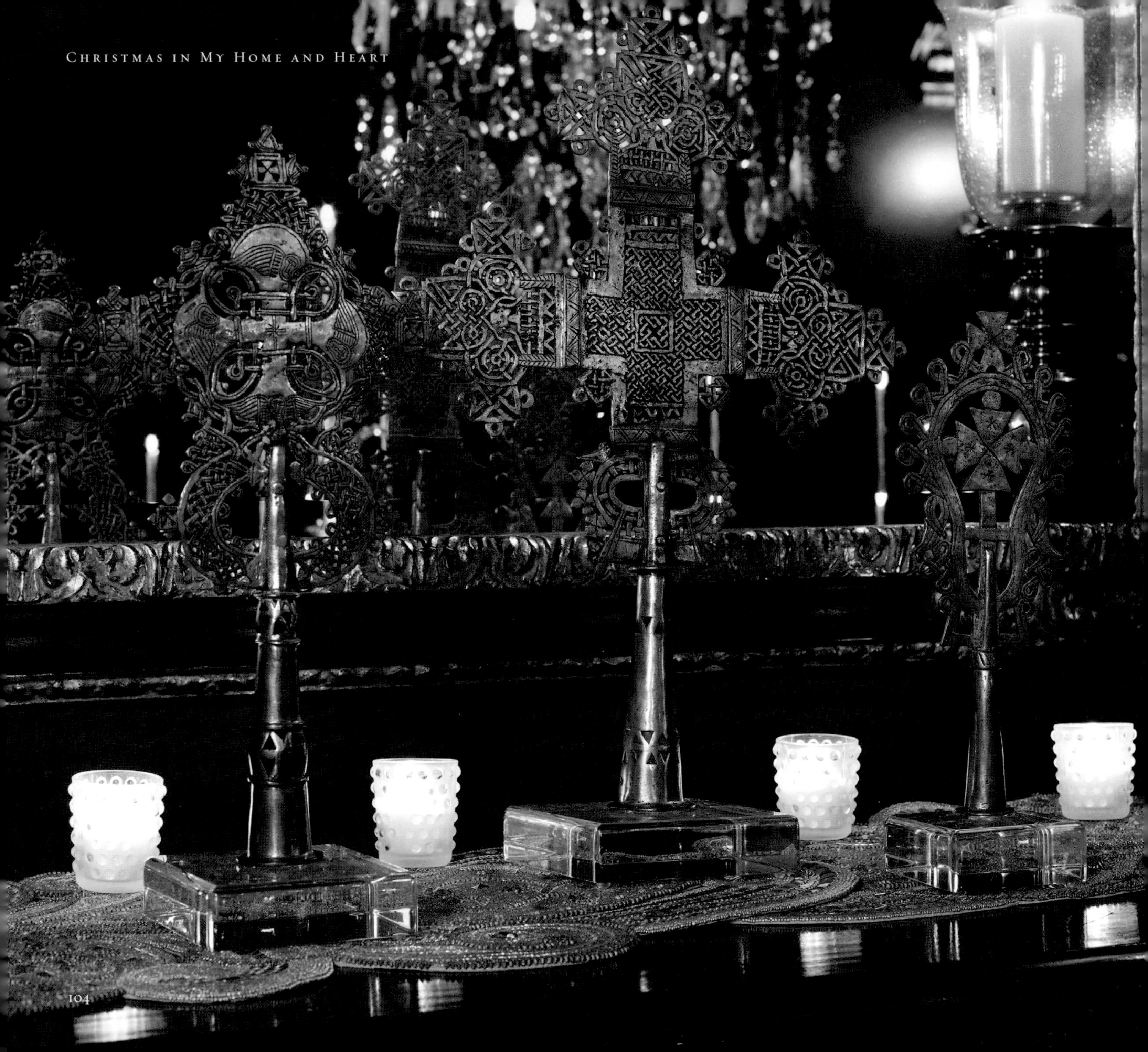

Before each day gets hectic and filled with activities, I make sure I devote time to prayer. Prayer is the most important thing I could ever offer to anyone—more important than the grandest party, more than the best gifts. Prayer is what will really make a lasting difference in the lives of those around me. Prayer also makes a difference in my life in that I'm more refreshed and renewed spiritually and more able to stay true to what's important to me.

We've spent a lot of time traveling the world and have come to truly enjoy the splendor of churches in other countries. When my sister Cindi had that horrific accident—when she was doused in acid—it was so shocking to experience, I prayed constantly for her full recovery. I knew that it would be a long road to healing and that our faith as a family would have to help her and us through. That year we visited Paris, France, and visited the Notre Dame Cathedral. While we were there, we lit a candle and again prayed for holy assistance. Though it has been a long road, Cindi is not only doing well, but she lives as an amazing example of true grace and forgiveness.

Each year Phillip would do what he called his Christmas Interview. We'd put Christmas hats on the boys and have them sit in a rocking chair next to the tree. Then Phillip would set up the video camera and interview them about their past year: who was their favorite teacher, what were some special events, things like that. The year Jordan was born, Jay held him in his lap while Phillip taped the interview. I cannot tell you how special and fun it's been to watch those videos every year! And they will be wonderful keepsakes for the boys to show their kids someday.

After doing the Christmas Interview, Phillip and I would read aloud the Christmas story from the gospel of Luke and then put the boys to bed.

Every Christmas Eve, after everyone's in bed and all the festivities have died down, I love to sit, look at the tree, and reflect on all that fills my heart, all that I am thankful for, and the real reason behind all of the celebrations. Then this one time of the year, I have a tradition of keeping all of the lights in the garland and trees on all night so that when we wake up in the morning, they're all lit to greet us into the new day—Christ's birthday.

The day after Christmas all the decorations come down. As much as I love the season, it's not a sad time because the minute that last ornament is put away, I start looking forward to the next Christmas! I love every holiday we have throughout each year; I think they're all opportunities for families to be together and to create great memories, but Christmas . . . it's always been my favorite.

I hope this Christmas season—and every Christmas—you'll be able to pause and reflect on the passing year and anticipate the one ahead. I hope that you'll spend your Christmases loving on those around you, creating warm and pleasant spaces for your family and yourself and giving to those who have less than you. I wish that you'll learn to take time for yourself, that you'll enjoy the process leading up to Christmas, and that stress and pressure will not reign in your home. I hope you have opportunities to express your creativity, welcome all around you, eat delicious food, and laugh until your belly hurts! And most of all, I pray that God will richly bless you and that you will know and be thankful for His precious gift to us, the gift of His Son, and the reason we celebrate this joyous time.

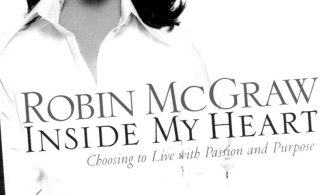

#1 NEW YORK TIMES BESTSELLER

ROBIN McGRAW
INSIDE MY HEART

Choosing to Live with Passion and Purpose

In *Inside My Heart*, Robin speaks directly to the heart of every woman and challenges her to recognize and develop her unique role to lead her to satisfaction with herself, her profession, her family, and anything she strives after.

ISBN 978-0-7852-1836-4

Times Best-Selling Author *Robin McGraw*

ROBIN McGRAW
INSIDE MY HEART

Choosing to Live with Passion and Purpose

GUIDED JOURNAL

ISBN 978-1-4185-1436-5

In the *Inside My Heart Guided Journal*, Robin McGraw, wife of the celebrated Dr. Phil, builds on the precepts of the "Dr. Phil Show" but speaks directly to the heart of every woman. She challenges women to recognize and develop their unique roles that lead them to satisfaction with themselves, their profession, their family, and anything they want to achieve.

WHAT'S AGE GOT TO DO WITH IT?

55

LIVING YOUR HAPPIEST & HEALTHIEST LIFE

ISBN 978-1-4002-0214-0

M ost women dread the thought of getting older. They're led to believe that once past a certain age, the greatest goal is avoiding wrinkles. In a culture gaga over beauty and youth, women hear the implicit message, "You are past your prime." But Robin McGraw is here to say that is absolutely not true!

In *What's Age Got to Do with It?*, Robin reclaims what it means to be, act, and feel young, showing women how to choose a vibrant life of meaning and satisfaction at any age. Diving into subjects like identity, relationships, lifestyle choices, and many others, Robin takes readers on a high-energy ride to living like they never have before.

BEST-SELLING AUTHOR *Robin McGraw*

#1 *NEW YORK TIMES* BEST-SELLING AUTHOR

ROBIN MCGRAW

ROBIN McGRAW'S
COMPLETE MAKEOVER GUIDE

A COMPANION TO
WHAT'S AGE GOT TO DO WITH IT?

ISBN 978-1-4002-0251-5

This *Complete Makeover Guide* is for a woman like you. A woman who is ready to do what's best for today and tomorrow, for her family and herself. A woman who knows that nothing can change until she makes the first step. A woman resolved to put herself at the top of the priority list so she can positively impact the lives of those she loves.

In the pages of this interactive companion book, you will find all you need to get your health and happiness journey underway.

You can look and feel your best no matter what age. And Robin McGraw's *Complete Makeover Guide*, the companion book to *What's Age Got to Do with It?*, will help you get there. Now let's get started!